The Story of the World

TEST BOOK AND ANSWER KEY

Volume 2: The Middle

Peace Hill Press
Charles City, Virginia
www.peacehillpress.com

How to Use These Tests and Answer Key

These Tests and their accompanying Answer Key are designed to go along with Volume 2 of Susan Wise Bauer's *The Story of the World: History for the Classical Child*. These tests are designed for those teachers and parents who want to evaluate their students' understanding of the major ideas and dates found within the *Story of the World* text. After your student reads each chapter of the book, he should be given time to review the reading before taking that chapter's test. If you are using the *Story of the World Volume 2 Activity Book*, you should go through the chapter's Review Questions, Narration Exercises, Map Activities, and other complementary projects and readings. These will reinforce and expand your student's knowledge of the material. For more information on the *Volume 2 Activity Book*, please visit www.peacehillpress.com. We recommend reading one chapter of the text each week and taking the appropriate test at the end of the week.

Although *The Story of the World* is intended for students between grades 1 and 6, we recommend that these tests be used with students in grade 3 and up. They can be used with younger students, but you might find that the Review Questions in the Activity Book are sufficient for evaluating your student's comprehension. For more ideas, support, and suggestions, visit the *Well-Trained Mind* message boards, at www.welltrainedmind/forums.

Photocopying and Distribution Policy

The tests and answer key in this book are copyrighted material owned by Peace Hill Press. Please do not reproduce any part of this material on e-mail lists or websites.

Families: You may make as many photocopies of these tests as you need for use WITHIN YOUR OWN FAMILY ONLY.

Schools and co-ops MAY NOT PHOTOCOPY any portion of the test book. We offer a reprinting license, of $1 per student, per test book, per year. If you would like to purchase this reprinting license, please contact Peace Hill Press: e-mail info@peacehillpress.com; phone 1.877.322.3445.

Name _____   Date _____

Chapter 24 Test: The Ottoman Empire

A. Fill in the blanks.

1. The Turks were a ragged band of nomads who wandered through central _____, hunting for food and fighting with their neighbors.

2. The king of the Ottoman Turks was known as the _____.

3. _____ the Conqueror finally captured Constantinople.

4. Constantinople was renamed _____ by the Ottoman Turks.

5. The greatest leader of the Ottoman Turks, Suleiman, declared that he was the_____ _____, the head of all the Muslims in the entire world.

B. Multiple Choice. Circle the letter of the best choice.

6. What happened to the Turks when they began trading with Muslim merchants?

    a. They became Muslims themselves.

    b. They decided to go to China to trade.

    c. They wanted to convert the Muslims to Christianity.

    d. They started a war with the Muslims.

7. The Turks finally settled down on the edge of _____.

    a. China

    b. the Byzantine Empire

    c. Arabia

    d. the Mongolian Empire

8. When the Turks settled down, many became _____.

    a. priests

    b. farmers and shepherds

    c. sailors

    d. merchants

9. What new weapon did the Ottoman Turks use to attack Constantinople?

    a. warships

    b. catapults

    c. gunpowder

    d. scimitars

10. What is a mercenary?

    a. a devout Muslim warrior

    b. a paid soldier from another country

    c. a type of sword used by the Turks

    d. a weapon used by the people of Constantinople

11. What did Suleiman do to unite his kingdom and make sure everyone was treated fairly?

    a. He used the same laws once used by King Solomon.

    b. He divided all the wealth equally among the people.

    c. He allowed the people to govern themselves.

    d. He made one set of laws for everyone to follow.

12. Suleiman rebuilt the walls around _____ after he had a dream.

    a. Jerusalem

    b. Constantinople

    c. Mecca

    d. Medina

13. Suleiman's son was known as _____.

    a. The Magnificent

    b. The Drunkard

    c. Slave of God

    d. Master of the World

C. True or False. Write "true" or "false."

_____ 14. In the story of the thirsty shepherd, Allah turned the shepherd into a sheep.

_____ 15. As the Ottoman Empire grew, the Byzantine Empire shrank.

_____ 16. A lunar eclipse convinced the Byzantines that they would be defeated.

_____ 17. Suleiman had the largest spy network in the world.

_____ 18. All Muslims agreed that Suleiman should be their spiritual leader.

D. Answer the following question using complete sentences.

19. Why is the conquest of Constantinople sometimes called the End of the Middle Ages?

_____

_____

_____

_____

Name _____   Date _____

The Story of the World

Chapter 26 Test: France and England at War

A.   Fill in the blanks.

1.   France and England fought for many years in the _____
_____ War.

2.   Henry V was made famous by a play written by _____.

3.   While Henry V ruled England, _____ ruled France.

4.   His son was the French prince or the _____.

B.   Multiple Choice. Circle the letter of the best choice.

5.   What did Henry V demand of the French king?

    a. land

    b. the king's daughter for a wife

    c. money

    d. a & b

6.   What did the French prince send with his message to Henry?

    a. his sister

    b. tennis balls

    c. gold

    d. nothing

7.   What happened when Henry's army first landed in France?

    a. He quickly defeated the French in several battles.

    b. His army was crushed in a large battle with the French.

    c. His soldiers deserted him.

    d. His soldiers became sick, and their shoes began to wear out.

8. What happened at the Battle of Agincourt?

      a. The French drove the English out of France.

      b. The English won even though the French army was much bigger.

      c. Henry V proved that he was a coward.

      d. The French prince gave a famous speech to rally his troops.

9. Who became the ruler of England and France after both kings died?

      a. the French prince

      b. the one-year-old son of Henry V

      c. the wife of Henry V

      d. Charles VII

10. Why were the people of France divided in a civil war?

      a. They could not agree about who should be the new king.

      b. They did not all speak the same language.

      c. They practiced different religions.

      d. all of the above

11. The two sides were fighting over the city of _____.

      a. Burgundy

      b. Orleans

      c. Paris

      d. Rheims

12. Who came to help the French prince protect this city?

      a. the Duke of Burgundy

      b. Joan of Arc

      c. Henry VI

      d. Charles VII

13. Who finally won the civil war?

> a. the Duke of Burgundy
>
> b. Joan of Arc
>
> c. Henry VI
>
> d. Charles VII

C. True or False. Write "true" or "false."

_____ 14. As the Black Death swept across Europe, the French and the English continued to fight.

_____ 15. Some French people wanted an English king because they thought the English would give them land and money.

_____ 16. Joan of Arc claimed that God sent her a vision telling her to lead the French into battle.

_____ 17. When Joan of Arc was captured, the French prince tried to rescue her.

D. Answer the following questions using complete sentences.

18. Who captured Joan of Arc? What was she tried for? How did she die?

_____

_____

_____

_____

Name _____ Date _____

The Story of the World

Chapter 28 Test: The Kingdoms of Spain and Portugal

A. Fill in the blanks.

1. Spain was divided into three kingdoms. _____ and_____ were two large kingdoms, and _____was a smaller kingdom on the western coast.

2. _____ and _____ combined their two kingdoms into one large kingdom of Spain.

3. Prince Henry of Portugal became known as Henry the _____.

B. Multiple Choice. Circle the letter of the best choice.

4. What did King Enrique promise the famous fighter Pedro Giron if Pedro would send men for the king's army?

    a. thousands of pounds of gold

    b. protection from the Moors

    c. his sister's hand in marriage

    d. a place in the Spanish court

5. What happened to Pedro Giron?

    a. He was killed by King Enrique.

    b. He died fighting the Moors.

    c. He died of stomach pains.

    d. He married the king's sister.

6. When King Enrique wanted his sister to marry the king of Portugal, she _____.

    a. killed herself

    b. sent a message to another prince

    c. became a nun

    d. killed her brother

7. _____ was the last kingdom of Spain to be under Muslim rule.

    a. Alhambra

    b. Valencia

    c. Seville

    d. Granada

8. How long did it take the rulers of Spain to drive the Moors out of this kingdom?

    a. one year

    b. ten years

    c. five years

    d. twenty years

9. After the Moors were gone, what did the rulers of Spain do?

    a. They made it illegal to practice any religion other than Christianity.

    b. They killed all of the Jews living in Spain.

    c. They attacked Portugal.

    d. all of the above

10. What did Prince Henry want to do?

    a. He wanted to make the Portuguese into great sailors and explorers.

    b. He wanted to conquer the kingdom of Spain.

    c. He wanted to become the next king of Portugal.

    d. all of the above

11. What kinds of goods did the merchants from Africa have to trade?

    a. olives, grapes, and tripe

    b. ivory, gold, and salt

    c. pepper, cloves, and nutmeg

    d. weapons, fruit, and exotic animals

12. What kinds of goods did the merchants from India have to trade?

     a. olives, grapes, and tripe

     b. ivory, gold, and salt

     c. pepper, cloves, and nutmeg

     d. weapons, fruit, and exotic animals

C. True or False. Write "true" or "false."

_____ 13. Spices were important in the Middle Ages because there were no refrigerators to keep meat from going bad.

_____ 14. An astrolabe is an instrument with a magnetic needle that always points north.

_____ 15. The Portuguese were excited about sailing through unfamiliar waters.

_____ 16. Prince Henry discovered a new route to trade with India.

D. Answer the following question using complete sentences.

17. Why were the Portuguese so interested in building and sailing boats?

_____

_____

_____

_____

Name _____ Date _____

The Story of the World

Chapter 29 Test: African Kingdoms

A. Fill in the blanks.

1. It was difficult to travel into southern Africa because the _____ Desert blocked the way.

2. In _____ Africa, many Africans lived in kingdoms with houses, roads, palaces, and schools.

3. The Europeans called Ghana the Land of _____.

4. The most famous of all Mali kings was _____.

5. _____ was the best-known city in the kingdom of Songhay.

B. Multiple Choice. Circle the letter of the best choice.

6. Ghana became rich and powerful by _____.

   a. trading salt and gold to the Europeans

   b. stealing salt and gold from neighboring tribes

   c. taxing the salt and gold that traveled through it

   d. digging gold out of the ground by chipping thousands of short shafts

7. Why did African Muslims attack the cities of Ghana?

   a. The Muslims wanted Ghana's gold.

   b. The kings of Ghana refused to convert to Islam.

   c. The Muslims were tired of paying taxes to the kings of Ghana.

   d. all of the above

8. Who brought Islam to the kingdom of Mali?

   a. traders

   b. warriors who attacked Ghana

   c. missionaries

   d. slaves captured from Muslim lands

9. How did the famous king of Mali attract the attention of the whole world?

    a. He gathered the largest army in all of Africa.

    b. He conquered neighboring kingdoms to expand the kingdom of Mali.

    c. He became the richest king in all of Africa.

    d. He made a pilgrimage to Mecca.

10. The kingdom of Songhay was famous for its _____.

    a. salt and gold

    b. great kings

    c. great size

    d. schools and libraries

11. Who was Leo Africanus?

    a. the king of Songhay

    b. a traveler who wrote a book about his travels

    c. a famous Muslim warrior

    d. the sultan of Morocco

12. Who invaded the kingdom of Songhay?

    a. the Ottoman Empire

    b. Portugal

    c. Spain

    d. Morocco

C. **True or False. Write "true" or "false."**

_____ 13. Africa was called the Dark Continent because almost no one had traveled down into Africa.

_____ 14. "Working in the salt mines" means making a fortune off of just a little work.

_____ 15. The kings of Mali built schools so that people could learn to read the Koran.

_____ 16. When travelers in the desert could not find water, they would sometimes kill their camels and squeeze water out of their bodies.

_____ 17. Books were the most valuable possession in the kingdom of Ghana.

D. **Answer the following question using complete sentences.**

18. How did the people of Mali show respect for their king?

_____

_____

_____

_____

The Story of the World

Chapter 30 Test: India Under the Moghuls

A. **Matching. Match each name with the correct description.**

____ 1. Babur

a. a famous ruler of India who is the subject of many stories

____ 2. Gupta

b. the first king who began to unite smaller kingdoms in India

____ 3. Chandragupta

c. given the nickname "the Tiger" because of his courage

____ 4. Humayan

d. fell and hit his head on the steps of his library

____ 5. Akbar

e. the dynasty that ruled India during the Golden Age of India

B. **Multiple Choice. Circle the letter of the best choice.**

6. Babur was from the empire of the _____.

   a. Gupta

   b. Ottoman Turks

   c. Huns

   d. Mongols

7. Babur was descended from _____.

   a. Genghis Khan

   b. Chandragupta

   c. Attila the Hun

   d. Akbar

8. What city did Babur invade?

   a. Bengal

   b. Agra

   c. Hindustan

   d. Delhi

9. Why were the sultan's war elephants defeated?

    a. They were outnumbered by Babur's horses.

    b. They were slow and ponderous.

    c. Babur's soldiers shot them with bows and arrows.

    d. The sultan did not have enough men to ride them.

10. What did Babur do when he became the new emperor?

    a. He killed all of the Hindus.

    b. He closed all of the schools.

    c. He made sure that laws were followed.

    d. all of the above

11. Akbar was Babur's _____.

    a. son

    b. grandson

    c. father

    d. nephew

12. What did Akbar do to be popular with his people?

    a. He married a Hindu princess.

    b. He made up folk tales about himself.

    c. He built beautiful gardens.

    d. He made all of the Hindus leave.

13. How big was Akbar's empire?

    a. It included all of India.

    b. It covered half of India.

    c. It was smaller than Babur's empire.

    d. It stretched from the Ottoman Empire all the way to China.

C.   True or False. Write "true" or "false."

_____   14.   While India was suffering from floods, famines, and disease, the Huns attacked.

_____   15.   Babur founded the Gupta dynasty.

_____   16.   Babur was known for being a fair and just ruler.

_____   17.   In many Indian stories, the emperor is guided by his state minister, Birbal.

_____   18.   In most of these stories, the emperor is too stubborn to listen to Birbal.

D.   Answer the following question using complete sentences.

19.   Describe the Garden of Scattered Flowers.

_____

_____

_____

_____

Name _____   Date _____

The Story of the World

Chapter 31 Test: Exploring New Worlds

A.   Matching. Match each explorer with the correct description.

____ 1.   da Gama   a.   He was the first adventurer to land in America.

____ 2.   Columbus   b.   His ship was the first to sail all the way around the world.

____ 3.   Vespucci   c.   He wanted to discover a new route to the east.

____ 4.   Magellan   d.   He was the first explorer to sail around Africa to reach India.

____ 5.   Ericsson   e.   He was the first explorer to realize that North America wasn't India.

B.   Multiple Choice. Circle the letter of the best choice.

6.   Columbus was a sailor from _____.

    a.   Portugal

    b.   Spain

    c.   Italy

    d.   France

7.   What did Columbus need before he could begin his journey?

    a.   money to pay for ships and supplies

    b.   the blessing of the king

    c.   maps of the Atlantic Ocean

    d.   a captain for his ship

8.   Who first decided to help Columbus?

    a.   the king of Portugal

    b.   Isabella of Spain

    c.   King Ferdinand

    d.   the king of France

9.   Why did many of the sailors get sick after they had been sailing for a long time?

     a.   They got seasick in the rough waters.

     b.   They were homesick and frightened.

     c.   They did not have enough fresh fruit or vegetables to eat.

     d.   One of the sailors had smallpox, which quickly spread.

10.   What kinds of gifts did the "Indians" bring to Columbus?

     a.   salt and gold

     b.   nutmeg and pepper

     c.   many kinds of jewels

     d.   cotton thread, parrots, and sweet potatoes

11.   Why did more people read about Vespucci's travels than the voyage of Columbus?

     a.   Columbus was killed before his ship returned home.

     b.   Vespucci was more popular with the king and queen.

     c.   Vespucci published many accounts of his travels.

     d.   all of the above

12.   This new part of the world was named after _____.

     a.   Columbus

     b.   da Gama

     c.   Magellan

     d.   Vespucci

C.   True or False. Write "true" or "false."

_____   13.   As Columbus left the harbor, he passed ships loaded with Jews leaving Spain.

_____   14.   Columbus sailed with three ships named the Niña, the Pinta, and the Santa Teresa.

_____   15.   Many people thought Columbus would run out of food and water before he reached the end of his journey.

_____   16.   Vespucci was the explorer who named the Pacific Ocean.

_____   17.   Magellan was looking for a river to cut through South America, but he never found one.

D. Answer the following question using complete sentences.

18. Why were explorers so interested in finding a new way to get to India?

_____

_____

_____

_____

The Story of the World

Chapter 32 Test: The American Kingdoms

A. Fill in the blanks.

1. The bridge of land that links North America and South America together is called

    _____.

2. The Mayans lived on the _____ Peninsula, which lies between the Gulf of Mexico and the Caribbean Sea.

3. Tenochtitlan was a great city built by the _____.

4. Huayna Capac was a great king of the _____.

5. The Incas lived in an area that is today called _____.

B. Multiple Choice. Circle the letter of the best choice.

6. Who lived in the Mayan cities?

    a. everyone

    b. farmers

    c. craftsmen

    d. kings and noblemen

7. What did the Mayan kings do to look "godlike"?

    a. paint their faces

    b. file their teeth

    c. have pointed heads and crossed eyes

    d. all of the above

8. What did the Mayan king have to do before a battle?

    a. sacrifice his children

    b. shed his own blood

    c. fast and pray

    d. play the Mayan ball game

9. Why did the Aztecs decide to build a city in the middle of a lake?

   a. They thought the sun god told them to build there.

   b. They wanted to have plenty of drinking water for their city.

   c. They thought it would be easier to protect from enemies.

   d. They followed an eagle to the lake.

10. How did the Aztecs get their food?

   a. They stole food from people living around the lake.

   b. They grew crops on top of the lake.

   c. They bought food from their enemies.

   d. all of the above

11. What new kind of food did the Aztecs learn how to make?

   a. chocolate

   b. sweet potatoes

   c. beer

   d. green peppers

12. What kinds of goods did the Incas trade?

   a. chocolate and gold

   b. cloth, pottery, and jewelry

   c. wool and llamas

   d. sweet potatoes and jewelry

13. Why was the Incan empire so weak when the Spanish explorers arrived?

   a. They had been attacked by the Aztecs.

   b. They did not have good roads throughout the kingdom.

   c. The kingdom had been divided, and the two rulers were fighting with each other.

   d. They had just endured several earthquakes and famines.

C. True or False. Write "true" or "false."

_____ 14. The empires in the Americas fought with each other, just like the empires over in Europe and Asia.

_____ 15. The Mayans limited the power of the king, just as the nations in Europe did.

_____ 16. The Aztecs were well-liked by their neighboring tribes.

_____ 17. According to legend, Manco Capac was the son of the Incan sun god.

_____ 18. The Incan governors sent messages to each other using knots on a rope.

D. Answer the following question using complete sentences.

19. Why did the Mayan cities crumble away into the jungle?

_____

_____

_____

_____

Name _____ Date _____

The Story of the World

Chapter 33 Test: Spain, Portugal, and the New World

A. Fill in the blanks.

1. The _____ are islands just off South America.

2. The Spanish and Portuguese sent soldiers called _____ to attack the people who lived in Central and South America.

3. The long journey that slaves were forced to take from West Africa to Central and South America is called the _____.

4. Hernán Cortés was a Spanish explorer who was looking for a city of _____.

5. Cortés met _____, the king of the Aztecs.

B. Multiple Choice. Circle the letter of the best choice.

6. Why did Ferdinand and Isabella pay for explorers to go to America?

    a. They were still looking for a better route to India.

    b. They hoped to make money and find treasure.

    c. They were running out of land to farm in Spain.

    d. They wanted to spread Christianity to the people in America.

7. What deal did Spain and Portugal make?

    a. They promised to share all of the gold they found in the New World.

    b. They agreed to join together to fight the Aztecs, the Mayans, and the Incas.

    c. They decided to divide the land in Central and South America.

    d. all of the above

8. What were the Spanish and Portuguese lacking for their new settlements?

    a. weapons to protect themselves from the natives

    b. safe water to drink

    c. materials to build houses and cities

    d. people to grow crops and mine gold

9.   The Spanish and Portuguese first got slaves from _____.

      a. West African kings

      b. Muslim traders

      c. the Aztecs

      d. the Mayans

10.   Why were the Aztecs so frightened of Cortés and his men?

      a. They had never seen horses.

      b. Cortés and his men wore strange masks.

      c. They had never seen boats.

      d. all of the above

11.   Who did the king of the Aztecs think Cortés was?

      a. a god

      b. the king of Portugal

      c. the king of Spain

      d. his dead father

12.   What did Cortés do after he escaped from Tenochtitlan?

      a. He killed himself.

      b. He went back to Spain.

      c. He paid some Indians to kill the king of the Aztecs.

      d. He gathered a fresh army and marched back to the city.

C. True or False. Write "true" or "false."

_____ 13. Sometimes in Africa, poor men would sell themselves as slaves so that their families could have more money.

_____ 14. African kings would capture enemy soldiers and sell them as slaves.

_____ 15. In Africa, slaves were never given a chance to buy back their freedom.

_____ 16. Europeans believed that all people were created equal by God.

_____ 17. The Aztecs welcomed Cortés by giving him gifts made of gold.

_____ 18. Cortés became the governor of the new Spanish colony in South America.

D. Answer the following question using complete sentences.

19. How did the Spanish and Portuguese treat the people of Central and South America?

_____

_____

_____

_____

The Story of the World

Chapter 34 Test: Martin Luther's New Ideas

A. Fill in the blanks.

1. The time when countries began to send ships to lands far away is known as the Age of _____
    _____.

2. A _____ is a new settlement in a land far away.

3. Martin Luther wrote a list called the _____
    _____, which explained why indulgences were wrong.

4. He nailed his list to the church door at _____.

5. Henry VIII started a new church known as the _____
    _____.

B. Multiple Choice. Circle the letter of the best choice.

6. Martin Luther's parents wanted him to be a lawyer, but he became a _____.

    a. priest

    b. teacher

    c. monk

    d. doctor

7. Martin Luther was afraid that _____.

    a. the pope would be angry at him for his new ideas

    b. God would punish him for his sins if he didn't do certain things

    c. people wouldn't like him if he shared his ideas

    d. all of the above

8. What Catholic church practice greatly upset Martin Luther?

    a. praying the Lord's Prayer

    b. paying money to the church to get out of doing penance for sin

    c. reading the Bible

    d. praying in front of the relics of the saints

9. Whom did Henry VII arrange for his son, Arthur, to marry?

    a. a German princess

    b. an English lady-in-waiting

    c. the queen of Spain

    d. the daughter of the king of Spain

10. Why did Henry VIII break from the Catholic church and start his own church?

    a. He wanted to spread the ideas of Martin Luther.

    b. The pope would not allow him to marry his brother's widow.

    c. The pope would not give him permission to marry again.

    d. The pope criticized Henry's choice for a wife.

11. How many wives did Henry VIII have in all?

    a. four

    b. five

    c. six

    d. seven

12. Why was Henry VIII unhappy with so many of his wives?

    a. He thought they were all ugly.

    b. They could not give him a son to be his heir.

    c. They argued with him about his new church.

    d. They spent too much of his money.

C. True or False. Write "true" or "false."

_____ 13. Martin Luther preached that God would forgive any sinner who believed in Jesus Christ.

_____ 14. Henry VII was anxious to make sure that his son would inherit the English throne because he did not want another war to start when he died.

_____ 15. The English noblemen supported Henry when he broke away from the Catholic church because they did not like the pope.

_____ 16. Henry VIII beheaded two of his wives.

_____ 17. Henry VIII never had the son he so desperately wanted.

D. Answer the following question using complete sentences.

18. How did Martin Luther's way of thinking change when he studied the book of Romans?

_____

_____

_____

_____

Name _____   Date _____

Chapter 35 Test: The Renaissance

A. Fill in the blanks.

1. When the Ottoman Turks conquered Constantinople, many Eastern Orthodox Christian scholars took scrolls written in _____ with them as they left the city.

2. The word "Renaissance" means "_____."

3. Observing something and then drawing conclusions from your observations is known as the____
_____.

4. The _____ changed the world more than any other invention.

5. It was invented by _____.

B. Multiple Choice. Circle the letter of the best choice.

6. Why did the people who lived in countries such as England, France, Spain, and Italy have more time to think, read and study?

    a. They had slaves to do their work for them.

    b. They did not worry about daily chores such as farming, cooking, and cleaning.

    c. They didn't have to worry constantly about barbarian invasion.

    d. all of the above

7. What did the Eastern Orthodox scholars teach the people of Europe?

    a. how to read ancient languages

    b. how to worship God in a new way

    c. how to dress like people did in ancient civilizations

    d. how to fight like a Greek warrior

8. During the Middle Ages, how were books made?

    a. Monks made them by hand.

    b. Slaves were forced to copy them.

    c. People would go to a library and copy the book they wanted.

    d. There were no books in the Middle Ages.

9. During the Middle Ages, manuscripts were written on _____.

    a. parchment

    b. leather

    c. paper

    d. newsprint

10. The Chinese learned to make paper using _____.

    a. animal skins

    b. bark, straw, and old rags

    c. leaves

    d. linen

11. What was the first book to be printed using the new invention?

    a. a book of poetry

    b. Homer's *The Iliad*

    c. a science manual

    d. the Bible

12. William Caxton published books about _____.

    a. history

    b. poetry

    c. how to play chess

    d. all of the above

C. True or False. Write "true" or "false."

_____   13. During the Renaissance, art became less realistic than it was before the Renaissance.

_____   14. During the Renaissance, builders designed their buildings with Greek columns and Roman arches.

_____   15. Before the Renaissance, most families had their own copy of the Bible.

_____   16. Books helped scientists because now they could read about what other scientists had already discovered.

_____   17. Most priests could not read the Scriptures very well before the Renaissance.

D. Answer the following question using complete sentences.

18. How did the Renaissance change the way that people thought about the world?

_____

_____

_____

_____

The Story of the World

Chapter 36 Test: Reformation and Counter Reformation

A. Matching. Match each term with the correct definition.

_____ 1. penance   a. people who wanted the church to change

_____ 2. indulgences   b. men who no longer followed the truth about God

_____ 3. Reformers   c. those who argued against practices of the Catholic church

_____ 4. heretics   d. acts to show repentance

_____ 5. politics   e. the ways in which earthly rulers control their kingdoms

_____ 6. Protestants   f. something you could buy to avoid doing penance

B. Multiple Choice. Circle the letter of the best choice.

7. When Martin Luther criticized indulgences, he was really saying that the Catholic church _____.

     a. wasn't Christian

     b. worshiped a false god

     c. didn't always know what God wanted

     d. was breaking the Ten Commandments

8. Martin Luther thought people should _____ to find out what God was saying to them.

     a. ask a priest

     b. read the Bible

     c. go to church

     d. send a letter to the pope

9. A scholar named Philip Melanchthon wrote down the teachings of the Reformers in a document called the _____.

    a. Augsburg Reformation

    b. Wittenberg Confession

    c. Ninety-five Theses

    d. Augsburg Confession

10. Why did kings like Henry VIII think the Reformation was a good idea?

    a. They wanted to read the Bible for themselves.

    b. They wanted to do what they believed God was telling them to do.

    c. They didn't like an Italian pope telling them what to do.

    d. all of the above

11. Why did the pope call for a council to meet at Trent?

    a. to discuss the beliefs of the Catholic church

    b. to elect a new pope

    c. to gather an army to attack the Reformers

    d. to discipline Martin Luther

12. How long did the Council of Trent last?

    a. eighteen days

    b. ten weeks

    c. ten years

    d. eighteen years

13. After the Council of Trent, men had to go to _____ to become priests.

    a. Rome

    b. seminaries

    c. the university

    d. public school

C. True or False. Write "true" or "false."

_____ 14. Martin Luther's Ninety-five Theses were printed by printing presses and passed around to thousands of people.

_____ 15. Everyone agreed that translating the Bible into people's own languages was a good idea.

_____ 16. Baptists, Presbyterians, and Catholics are all known as Protestants.

_____ 17. During the Middle Ages, bishops and priests were sometimes landlords.

_____ 18. After the Counter Reformation, Catholics and Protestants got along better.

D. Answer the following question using complete sentences.

19. Why was the Catholic church worried about the ideas of the Reformers?

_____

_____

_____

_____

Name _____ Date _____

The Story of the World

Chapter 37 Test: The New Universe

A. **Fill in the blanks.**

1. Nicholas Copernicus grew up in the country of _____.

2. Copernicus is called the _____.

3. Galileo Galilei was born in the country of _____.

4. Einstein called Galileo the _____
    _____.

B. **Multiple Choice. Circle the letter of the best choice.**

5. The science of stars is called _____.

        a. astrology

        b. cosmotology

        c. astronomy

        d. geology

6. During Copernicus's time, most people believed that the _____ was/were at the center of the universe.

        a. sun

        b. Earth

        c. stars

        d. moon

7. This idea was based on the writings of the Egyptian astronomer, _____.

        a. Almagest

        b. Ptolemy

        c. Archimedes

        d. Aristarchus

8. According to Copernicus's new theory, the planets all revolved around the _____.

    a. sun

    b. Earth

    c. stars

    d. moon

9. When Galileo was in school, his teachers nicknamed him "the _____."

    a. Dreamer

    b. Arguer

    c. Clown

    d. Peacemaker

10. After observing a swinging chandelier, Galileo began to conduct experiments related to a force we now call _____.

    a. work

    b. speed

    c. gravity

    d. friction

11. Galileo also spent much of his time trying to figure out _____.

    a. how things work

    b. why the sun rises and sets

    c. why lightning occurs

    d. how matter is formed

12. Why do we consider Galileo one of the first modern scientists?

    a. He wrote down his ideas in a book.

    b. He tested his theories by performing experiments.

    c. He used the scientific method.

    d. He compared his ideas to the ideas of philosophers.

C. True or False. Write "true" or "false."

_____ 13. A star map shows where each star is at different times during the year.

_____ 14. Copernicus died the same year that his book, *On the Revolutions of the Heavenly Spheres*, was published.

_____ 15. Galileo believed that Copernicus's theory could be true.

_____ 16. Galileo invented the telescope.

_____ 17. The church supported Galileo and his theories.

D. Answer the following question using complete sentences.

18. Why was Copernicus afraid to publish his theory?

_____

_____

_____

_____

Name _____   Date _____

Chapter 38 Test: England's Greatest Queen

A. Fill in the blanks.

1.   Mary and Elizabeth were the daughters of _____.

2.   The English people's nickname for Mary was _____.

3.   Elizabeth was nicknamed _____.

4.   The group of representatives who helped the ruler of England make laws was called_____
   _____.

B. Multiple Choice. Circle the letter of the best choice.

5.   How old was Edward VI when his father died and he became king?

   a. six

   b. nine

   c. sixteen

   d. nineteen

6.   After Edward VI died, what was unusual about the next ruler of England?

   a. England had never had a ruler who was so young.

   b. The new ruler was not English.

   c. England had never had a woman on the throne before.

   d. The English people elected the new ruler.

7.   When Mary became queen, what did she do to Elizabeth?

   a. She tried to kill her.

   b. She had her imprisoned in the Tower of London.

   c. She sent her to live in another country.

   d. She made her a co-ruler.

8. Why was Mary so unpopular as queen?

    a. She demanded that people swear allegiance to the Catholic church.

    b. She married a foreign prince who helped her rule the country.

    c. She burned 300 men and women at the stake.

    d. all of the above

9. What do we call the years of Elizabeth's reign?

    a. the Elizabethan Age

    b. the Golden Age

    c. the Renaissance

    d. the Reformation

10. What did everyone want Elizabeth to do as soon as she became queen?

    a. expel the Catholics

    b. fight a war with Spain

    c. get married

    d. choose someone to be her heir

11. How was Elizabeth different from most Renaissance rulers?

    a. She did not keep any power for herself.

    b. She did not wear royal clothes and jewels.

    c. She did not make any alliances with other countries.

    d. She did not force her people to swear that they were Protestants or Catholics.

12. What did Elizabeth do as the ruler of England?

    a. She made alliances with other countries.

    b. She sent explorers out to claim undiscovered lands for England.

    c. She defended England against invasion.

    d. all of the above

C. True or False. Write "true" or "false."

_____ 13. When she was born, Mary was named the Princess of Wales, and she kept this title throughout her life.

_____ 14. When Mary died, the people of England sang and danced in the streets.

_____ 15. Elizabeth reigned in England for 65 years.

_____ 16. Mary's husband, Philip, offered to marry Elizabeth after Mary died.

_____ 17. During this time, most people thought women were wiser, smarter, and stronger than men.

D. Answer the following question using complete sentences.

18. Why was Elizabeth determined not to marry?

_____

_____

_____

_____

Name _____   Date _____

The Story of the World

Chapter 39 Test: England's Greatest Playwright

A. Fill in the blanks.

William Shakespeare wrote three different kinds of plays:

1. Funny plays are called _____.

2. An example of this type of play is _____.

3. A sad play is called a _____.

4. An example of this type of play is _____.

5. A play based on the life of a great man or woman in the past is an _____ play.

6. An example of this type of play is _____.

7. List a famous phrase from one of Shakespeare's plays. _____

_____

_____.

B. Multiple Choice. Circle the letter of the best choice.

8. How did Elizabeth entertain herself while she was queen?

    a. She kept a choir and orchestra at court.

    b. She sang and played the lyre.

    c. She wrote poetry and saw plays.

    d. all of the above

9. When Shakespeare was young he traveled in a company that _____.

    a. performed plays

    b. played music

    c. recited poetry

    d. sang songs

151

10. Where did this company perform?

    a. royal palaces

    b. great cathedrals

    c. wooden theatres and the courtyards of inns

    d. all of the above

11. Why did King Duncan give Macbeth the title "Thane of Cawdor"?

    a. Macbeth was his son.

    b. Macbeth had fought bravely for him.

    c. Lady Macbeth asked the king to give the title to her husband.

    d. Duncan was worried Macbeth would kill him if he didn't.

12. Who first told Macbeth that he would be the king of Scotland?

    a. Duncan

    b. Lady Macbeth

    c. Banquo

    d. three weird women

13. After Macbeth murdered Duncan, he told Lady Macbeth that he would never be able to _____.

    a. breathe

    b. rule the kingdom

    c. eat

    d. sleep

14. What did the army look like as they approached Macbeth's castle?

    a. a sea

    b. a forest

    c. invisible

    d. a mountain

C. True or False. Write "true" or "false."

_____ 15. William Shakespeare wrote more than forty plays.

_____ 16. Shakespeare's plays have never been translated into another language.

_____ 17. Lady Macbeth was more interested in Macbeth becoming king than he was.

_____ 18. Macbeth drugged the guards so that Lady Macbeth could kill the king.

_____ 19. Macbeth and Lady Macbeth both die at the end of the play.

D. Answer the following question using complete sentences.

20. What did Macbeth and Lady Macbeth do that showed they suffered from terrible guilt over what they had done?

_____

_____

_____

_____

Name _____ Date _____

Chapter 40 Test: New Ventures to the Americas

A. Fill in the blanks.

1. The first English colony in the New World was named _____ after Queen Elizabeth.

2. The first colonists settled on an island called _____.

3. _____ was the first English baby born in the New World.

4. When John White finally managed to return to the colony, he found no people, only the word _____ carved in a tree.

B. Multiple Choice. Circle the letter of the best choice.

5. How did Queen Elizabeth plan to keep Spain from becoming more powerful?

   a. She sent an army to attack Spain.

   b. She planned English journeys to South America.

   c. She allowed pirates to attack Spanish ships.

   d. all of the above

6. Elizabeth put Sir Walter Raleigh in charge of _____.

   a. attacking Spain

   b. exploring North America

   c. entertaining her

   d. raising money to pay for war

7. When the first English ships returned from North America, what did they bring?

   a. animal skins and tobacco

   b. pearls and gold

   c. timber and tools

   d. corn and potatoes

8. Why did the first colonists want to go home?

    a. They were tired of fighting with the Spanish.

    b. They were afraid of catching diseases from the Indians.

    c. It was cold and they had very little food.

    d. They couldn't find any gold.

9. Who stayed behind when the first colonists returned to England?

    a. John White

    b. John White's family

    c. Walter Raleigh

    d. fifteen soldiers

10. What finally happened to Walter Raleigh?

    a. He was killed by Queen Elizabeth.

    b. He was beheaded when he did not find gold in South America.

    c. He died in prison.

    d. He died while sailing to the New World.

11. Why did the Indians stop helping the colonists?

    a. The colonists told the Indians they did not need any help.

    b. The Indians were not getting paid for their help.

    c. The colonists attacked a group of friendly Indians by mistake.

    d. The leaders in England told the colonists to refuse help from the Indians.

12. What happened to the "Lost Colony?"

    a. They were killed by unfriendly Indians.

    b. They died of disease.

    c. They were captured by the Spanish.

    d. No one knows for sure.

C. True or False. Write "true" or "false."

_____ 13. In exchange for his work, Elizabeth promised Raleigh land in England.

_____ 14. Elizabeth liked Raleigh because he was charming, handsome, and poetic.

_____ 15. John White was forced to return to England because the colonists hated him.

_____ 16. White could not return to the colony right away because England was fighting in a war with Spain.

_____ 17. When White returned to the colony, he found that the houses had all burned.

D. Answer the following question using complete sentences.

18. Why was Queen Elizabeth so interested in North America?

_____

_____

_____

_____

The Story of the World

Chapter 41 Test: Explorations in the North

A. Fill in the blanks.

1. The _____ and the _____ created colonies in Central and South America.

2. The _____ settled in the land of Virginia.

3. _____ was the first explorer to reach Newfoundland.

4. He claimed this land for _____.

5. The first settlement on Newfoundland became known as _____.

6. Jacques Cartier named the land he saw _____ after the Micmac word for village.

B. Multiple Choice. Circle the letter of the best choice.

7. The first explorer who reached Newfoundland found a huge number of _____.

   a. Native Americans

   b. fish

   c. beaver

   d. all of the above

8. This explorer thought he had landed in _____.

   a. Asia

   b. India

   c. Iceland

   d. Greenland

9. Who were the first people to settle in Newfoundland?

    a. trappers

    b. farmers

    c. fishermen

    d. soldiers

10. What is a flake?

    a. a fisherman

    b. a wooden platform for salting & drying fish

    c. a fishing settlement

    d. a small fishing boat

11. Jacques Cartier was sent to explore North America by _____.

    a. the king of France

    b. the king of Spain

    c. Queen Elizabeth

    d. the king of Portugal

12. Cartier was hoping to find _____.

    a. gold & jewels

    b. a river that cut all the way across North America

    c. friendly Indians

    d. a new route to India

13. Why did Cartier make friends with the Micmac Indians?

    a. He wanted to find a guide to help him on his journey.

    b. He was hoping they would lead him to a great treasure.

    c. He didn't want them to attack him as he sailed down the river.

    d. He wanted to invite some of them to travel back to Europe with him.

14. What Indian tribe did Cartier meet next?

    a. the Mohicans

    b. the Powhatan

    c. the Hurons

    d. the Inuits

C. True or False. Write "true" or "false."

_____ 15. People from many different countries settled in Newfoundland.

_____ 16. The Micmac Indians lived in houses made of animal skins called wigwams.

_____ 17. Cartier took the two daughters of an Indian chief back with him to Europe.

_____ 18. Cartier was the first explorer to sail down the St. Lawrence River.

_____ 19. Cartier thought he had found a great treasure, but it turned out to be quartz.

D. Answer the following question using complete sentences.

20. Why didn't the first colonists stay in Newfoundland all year long?

_____

_____

_____

_____

Name _____   Date _____

Chapter 42 Test: Empires Collide

A. Fill in the blanks.

1. _____ had an empire so large that it was called "Mistress of the World and Queen of the Ocean."

2. Adventurers from _____ kept getting in the way of this powerful country.

3. The Spanish built a huge fleet of ships called the _____

    _____.

4. Sir _____

    was second in command of the navy that fought against the Spanish.

B. Multiple Choice. Circle the letter of the best choice.

5. How did the king of Spain get to be the king of England for a short time?

    a. He defeated the English at a major battle.

    b. He married the queen of England.

    c. He signed a peace treaty with England.

    d. He inherited the title when his father died.

6. Why did King Philip want to attack England?

    a. He was tired of English ships attacking Spanish ships.

    b. He wanted to prove that Spain was more powerful than England.

    c. He wanted to make England a Catholic country again.

    d. all of the above

7. Where did the battle between the English and Spanish ships take place?

    a. off the coast of Spain

    b. in the English Channel

    c. in the Atlantic Ocean

    d. off the coast of Newfoundland

8.   How did the English defeat Spanish ships?

     a.   They outnumbered the Spanish ships.

     b.   They shot the Spanish ships full of holes.

     c.   They surprised the Spanish by attacking at night.

     d.   They sailed up next to a Spanish ship, pulled the two ships together, and English soldiers poured over onto the Spanish ship and took it over.

9.   What did merchant ships hope to get from the Native Americans of Canada?

     a.   slaves

     b.   tobacco

     c.   spices

     d.   animal skins

10.   What did merchant ships take from Africa?

     a.   slaves and spices

     b.   gold, ivory, and slaves

     c.   animal skins

     d.   potatoes and wild animals

11.   The _____ Empire ruled over Istanbul and much of Arabia during the time of the explorers.

     a.   Moghul

     b.   Ottoman

     c.   Mali

     d.   Byzantine

12.   If you sailed down the coast of South America, you would see ruins of _____ temples and roads.

     a.   Aztec

     b.   Mayan

     c.   Huron

     d.   Incan

C. True or False. Write "true" or "false."

_____ 13. The kings of Japan were called samurai.

_____ 14. Foreigners were welcome in China during the Ming dynasty.

_____ 15. Explorers traveling to Newfoundland would find settlers fishing.

D. Answer the following question using complete sentences.

16. Why did the Spanish king become so annoyed by English ships?

_____

_____

_____

_____

The Story of the World, Volume 2: The Middle Ages
ANSWER KEY

Chapter 1 Test

1. Rome
2. Pax Romana
3. Celts
4. barbarians
5. Diocletian
6. a
7. d
8. b
9. c
10. c
11. b
12. true
13. false
14. false
15. false

16. If you visited ancient Rome, you might see people wearing togas walking along paved streets. You would see the Coliseum where gladiators fight and chariot races take place, and you might see marble columns with the statues of great Roman generals and emperors on top of them.

Chapter 2 Test

1. bards
2. Craith
3. Vortigern
4. Beowulf
5. b
6. b
7. a
8. d
9. c
10. b
11. a
12. c
13. false
14. false
15. true
16. true

17. This time period in England is known as the Dark Ages because the Angles and the Saxons didn't write down any history or records so we know very little about them.

Chapter 3 Test

1. pope
2. Augustine
3. Ethelbert
4. monasteries
5. a
6. c
7. a
8. d
9. b
10. a
11. b
12. b
13. true
14. true
15. false
16. false
17. true
18. false

19. Books were expensive during the Middle Ages because they were copied by hand and took months to make.

Chapter 4 Test

1. Constantinople
2. Byzantine Empire
3. Eastern Orthodox
4. patriarchs
5. a
6. d
7. b
8. c
9. c
10. a
11. d
12. b
13. false
14. true
15. true
16. false
17. true

18. Some of the laws from the Code of Justinian were everyone could go to the beach or the river; if you found treasure washed up by the river, you could keep it; you could own slaves; thieves must repay the owner of the stolen object; you must warn people below if you are trimming a tree near a road; preachers must be loud enough for everyone to hear.

Chapter 5 Test

1. c
2. d
3. b
4. e
5. a
6. b
7. d
8. a
9. d
10. d
11. a
12. b
13. c
14. false
15. true
16. false
17. true

18. The monks in India decorated their palaces by carving sculptures out of stone and painting frescoes on the walls.

Chapter 6 Test

1. Bedouins   2. Mecca   3. Muslims   4. Koran
5. b   6. a   7. c   8. a
9. b   10. a   11. c   12. d
13. true   14. false   15. true   16. false
17. true   18. true
19. The five pillars of Islam are Shahadah (faith), Salah (prayer), Zakat (giving), Sawm (fasting), and Hajj (pilgrimage).

Chapter 7 Test

1. caliphs   2. Baghdad   3. Sinbad   4. snakes   5. a
6. b   7. d   8. a   9. b   10. b
11. d   12. c   13. false   14. true   15. false
16. true
17. true
18. The new capital city of the Islamic Empire was Baghdad. It was known for its beautiful buildings, its running water, its public libraries, and its thinkers.

Chapter 8 Test

1. Yang Chien   2. Sui   3. Li Yuan   4. Tang   5. b
6. c   7. a   8. d   9. a   10. c
11. d   12. d   13. true   14. true   15. false
16. false   17. true   18. false
19. During the Golden Age of China, the Chinese learned how to print books. They also learned how to drain the sap from lacquer trees, color it, and paint it onto wood and cloth. Chinese scientists even learned how to make gunpowder.

Chapter 9 Test

1. clans   2. Yamato   3. Amaterasu   4. Rising Sun   5. c
6. a   7. c   8. a   9. b   10. c
11. d   12. b   13. true   14. false   15. true
16. false   17. false   18. false
19. Chinese customs came to Japan when the king of Paekche in Korea sent a book with Chinese letters in it to the emperor of Japan. The emperor was fascinated by the Chinese letters and wanted his son to learn how to read and write those letters. So the king of Paekche sent a tutor who taught the whole Japanese court how to read and write in Chinese. Soon all of the important people in Japan spoke Chinese and rich noblemen began to send their sons to China to study.

Chapter 10 Test

1. North America, South America, Antarctica, Africa, Europe, Asia, and Australia
2. nomads   3. Aborigines   4. Maori   5. c   6. a
7. b   8. c   9. a   10. b   11. c
12. false   13. true   14. true   15. false
16. The islands of New Zealand were formed when volcanoes rose out of the sea and their lava turned to stone.

Chapter 11 Test

1. Gaul   2. Troy   3. Merovius   4. Clovis   5. France
6. b   7. b   8. a   9. d   10. b
11. d   12. a   13. b   14. false   15. true
16. false   17. false
18. The four groups of people who lived in the Frankish Empire were the Franks, the Romans, the Burgundians, and the Allemani.

Chapter 12 Test

1. Visigoths
2. Berbers
3. Moors
4. Gibraltar
5. a
6. c
7. c
8. b
9. d
10. a
11. d
12. false
13. false
14. true
15. true
16. It was not a good idea to invite Tariq bin Ziyad to Spain because he did not want to help the king's sons get their throne back. He wanted to capture Spain for Islam.

Chapter 13 Test

1. Hammer
2. Tours
3. grandson
4. Emperor of the Romans
5. b
6. d
7. a
8. b
9. a
10. d
11. a
12. b
13. false
14. true
15. false
16. true
17. false
18. Charlemagne tried to improve the lives of his people by having more copies of the Scriptures made, building new roads and bridges, starting schools for boys, and teaching the people better ways to farm. He told families to bring their children to church, and he fought wars to expand his kingdom.

Chapter 14 Test

1. Scandinavia
2. Vikings
3. Normandy
4. Vineland
5. a
6. d
7. b
8. c
9. a
10. b
11. b
12. a
13. false
14. true
15. true
16. true
17. true
18. false
19. The Norsemen's ships were flat-bottomed boats. They were better than other boats because they could float in shallow water and could be rowed right up to the sand on a beach.

Chapter 15 Test

1 – 4. England, Wales, Scotland, Ireland
5. Celts
6. Anglo-Saxons
7. Vikings
8. b
9. c
10. b
11. c
12. a
13. b
14. b
15. a
16. false
17. true
18. false
19. true
20. false
21. The Vikings weren't Christians, so they didn't leave priests, monks, churches, and monasteries alone. They also kidnapped women and children.

Chapter 16 Test

1. Old English
2. Celtic
3. French
4. serfs
5. d
6. b
7. a
8. d
9. c
10. a
11. a
12. b
13. a
14. false
15. true
16. false
17. false
18. true
19. Feudalism is a way of living in which every person serves someone else and the person that he serves has a duty to give back something in exchange.

Chapter 17 Test

1. chivalry
2. tournaments
3. way of the warrior
4. haikus
5. b
6. c
7. d
8. b
9. c
10. b
11. a
12. d
13. c
14. false
15. true
16. false
17. false
18. true
19. Before becoming a knight, a boy would have to learn how to ride and how to fight with a sword. He would learn how to put on heavy armor and how to carry his shield properly. He would learn how to take care of a horse and how to clean the saddle and bridle. He would learn how to speak courteously and eat neatly, how to carve meat and serve it, and how to behave at a great feast.

Chapter 18 Test

1. Muslim or Islamic   2. pilgrim   3. Reconquest   4. El Cid   5. b
6. a   7. b   8. b   9. a   10. a
11. a   12. b   13. b   14. true   15. false
16. true   17. false   18. false
19. Jerusalem was an important city to the Muslims because they believed that Muhammad ascended to heaven from a rock inside the city. It was important to the Jews because it was the city of David and the ruins of the Temple were there. It was important to the Christians because Jesus was crucified there.

Chapter 19 Test

1. Lionhearted   2. Lackland   3. Magna Carta   4. Sherwood Forest   5. c
6. a   7. b   8. b   9. a   10. d
11. b   12. c   13. true   14. true   15. true
16. false
17. The Magna Carta meant that King John had to follow the law like everyone else.

Chapter 20 Test

1. Zealots   2. Torah   3. rabbis   4. synagogues   5. d
6. b   7. b   8. a   9. a   10. c
11. b   12. a   13. false   14. true   15. true
16. true
17. Yohanan thought that if the Jews studied the sacred writings of the Torah and continued to worship God in synagogues, they would still be Jews.

Chapter 21 Test

1. khans   2. Peking   3. Scourge   4. grandson   5. a
6. c   7. b   8. b   9. d   10. a
11. b   12. c   13. false   14. true   15. true
16. false   17. true
18. The Mongols were nomads who lived in tents. They wore furs and leather and rubbed their skin with grease to keep the wind away. They never settled down and grew crops. They could go for days at a time without food, and if they were in danger of starving, they would drink blood from their horses' veins.

Chapter 22 Test

1. Silk   2. father   3. Book of Marco   4. Forbidden City   5. b
6. c   7. a   8. c   9. a   10. a
11. b   12. d   13. false   14. false   15. true
16. true   17. false   18. false
19. The merchants who traveled to China found gold, cloves and ginger, jade and lacquer, rare and beautiful flowers, wine, sweet-smelling wood, rugs with rich complicated patterns, and silk.

Chapter 23 Test

1. Rurik   2. Slavs   3. Vladimir   4. Ivan the Great   5. tsar
6. c   7. a   8. a   9. b   10. b
11. a   12. c   13. b   14. false   15. true
16. false   17. true   18. true
19. Constantinople was hard to conquer because it was surrounded by water on three sides and the city had a moat and three walls around it. The walls had towers where archers could stand and shoot out to sea, and a chain was stretched across the water so ships couldn't get close to the shore.

Chapter 24 Test

1. Asia	2. sultan	3. Mehmed	4. Istanbul	5. Caliph
6. a	7. b	8. b	9. c	10. b
11. d	12. a	13. b	14. false	15. true
16. true	17. true	18. false		

19. The conquest of Constantinople is sometimes called the End of the Middle Ages because from that moment on, the way of life begun by the Romans centuries ago was truly over. The last remnants of the old Roman Empire had disappeared.

Chapter 25 Test

1. China	2. Black Death	3. bubonic	4. fleas, rats	5. d
6. d	7. a	8. a	9. a	10. b
11. b	12. c	13. true	14. true	15. true
16. false	17. false	18. false		

19. Because so many peasants died, noblemen couldn't find anyone to work on their land. The peasants who did survive could demand to be paid higher wages because they were in high demand. The noblemen's estates grew smaller and smaller because they could not afford to pay workers to farm all of their land and peasants earned more money and began to buy land of their own.

Chapter 26 Test

1. Hundred Years'	2. Shakespeare	3. Charles VI	4. Dauphin	5. d
6. b	7. d	8. b	9. b	10. a
11. b	12. b	13. d	14. false	15. true
16. true	17. false			

18. Joan of Arc was captured by the English and the Burgundians, but the French king did nothing to help her. The English and Burgundians put her on trial for witchcraft, and witnesses made up false stories about her. She was found guilty and burned to death.

Chapter 27 Test

1. Yorks, Lancastrians	2. Wars of the Roses	3. Protector	4. c	5. a
6. b	7. c	8. a	9. b	10. b
11. c	12. d	13. true	14. true	15. false
16. false	17. true			

18. The civil wars for the English throne were called the Wars of the Roses because the Yorks had a white rose on their banners and the Lancastrians had a red rose on their banners.

Chapter 28 Test

1. Castile, Aragon, Portugal		2. Ferdinand & Isabella		3. Navigator
4. c	5. c	6. b	7. d	8. b
9. a	10. a	11. b	12. c	13. true
14. false	15. false	16. false		

17. The Portuguese were interested in building and sailing boats because they had such a long coastline and they wanted to trade with other countries.

Chapter 29 Test

1. Sahara
2. West
3. Gold
4. Mansa Musa
5. Timbuktu
6. c
7. b
8. a
9. d
10. c
11. b
12. d
13. true
14. false
15. true
16. true
17. false
18. The people of Mali showed respect for their king by groveling in front of him. They wore dirty clothes and rolled up their trousers to their knees. They put their elbows, turbans, and hats on the ground, and they threw dust all over themselves the whole time the king was speaking.

Chapter 30 Test

1. c
2. e
3. b
4. d
5. a
6. b
7. a
8. d
9. b
10. c
11. b
12. a
13. b
14. false
15. false
16. true
17. true
18. false
19. Babur's Garden of Scattered Flowers had water wheels pulled by buffalo to water the garden. It had beds of beautiful flowers, cypress trees, and fruit trees. It also had marble benches where Babur could sit and think of his homeland.

Chapter 31 Test

1. d
2. c
3. e
4. b
5. a
6. c
7. a
8. b
9. c
10. d
11. c
12. d
13. true
14. false
15. true
16. false
17. false
18. Merchants wanted to travel to India to trade for spices, but there was no simple way to get there. To get spices, merchants had to make the long, rough journey over land. They had to fight off bandits and war bands, and they had to face the hostile Ottoman Turks.

Chapter 32 Test

1. Central America
2. Yucatan
3. Aztecs
4. Incas
5. Peru
6. d
7. d
8. b
9. a
10. b
11. a
12. b
13. c
14. true
15. false
16. false
17. true
18. true
19. The Mayan cities grew so big that the ground around them couldn't grow enough food to support all the city people. Hurricanes and earthquakes also wrecked many houses and temples. Many of the Mayan people were tired of their cruel and violent kings, and the Aztecs continued to attack the Mayan cities.

Chapter 33 Test

1. West Indies
2. conquistadores
3. Middle Passage
4. gold
5. Montezuma
6. b
7. c
8. d
9. b
10. a
11. a
12. d
13. true
14. true
15. false
16. false
17. true
18. false
19. The Spanish and the Portuguese marched into villages and cities and killed the people of Central and South America. They destroyed temples, houses, and palaces. They built Spanish settlements and claimed the land as their own.

Chapter 34 Test

1. Discovery or Exploration
2. colony
3. Ninety-five Theses
4. Wittenberg
5. Church of England
6. c
7. b
8. b
9. d
10. c
11. c
12. b
13. true
14. true
15. false
16. true
17. false
18. When Martin Luther studied the book of Romans, he realized that he didn't have to earn God's love by working hard to be good. He realized that God already loved him and would give him the power to be good.

Chapter 35 Test

1. Greek	2. rebirth	3. scientific method	4. printing press	5. Gutenberg
6. c	7. a	8. a	9. a	10. b
11. d	12. d	13. false	14. true	15. false
16. true	17. true			

18. During the Renaissance, people began to believe that they could find out truth by looking at the world and figuring out how it worked. They observed the world around them and then drew conclusions from what they observed.

Chapter 36 Test

1. d	2. f	3. a	4. b	5. e
6. c	7. c	8. b	9. d	10. c
11. a	12. d	13. b	14. true	15. false
16. false	17. true	18. false		

19. The Catholic church was worried about the ideas of the Reformers because if every man was his own priest, every man could come to his own conclusions about God. The Catholics worried that the Christian church would splinter in a hundred different pieces and then no one would know what the truth really was.

Chapter 37 Test

1. Poland	2. Father of Astronomy			
3. Italy	4. Father of Modern Physics			
5. c	6. b	7. b	8. a	9. b
10. c	11. a	12. b	13. true	14. true
15. true	16. false	17. false		

18. Copernicus was afraid to publish his theory because he was a devout Catholic. The Catholic church taught that, since man was the most wonderful part of God's creation, the earth must be at the center of creation because the earth is man's home. Copernicus was afraid that the leaders of the church would not approve of his new theory.

Chapter 38 Test

1. Henry VIII	2. Bloody Mary	3. Good Queen Bess	4. Parliament	5. b
6. c	7. b	8. d	9. a	10. c
11. d	12. d	13. false	14. true	15. false
16. true	17. false			

18. Elizabeth was determined not to marry because she knew that if she did, her husband would be the real ruler of England. Elizabeth did not want to give up any of her power, so she said that she was married to England.

Chapter 39 Test

1. comedies	2. examples include The Taming of the Shrew or A Midsummer Night's Dream
3. tragedy	4. examples include Hamlet or Romeo and Juliet or Macbeth
5. historical	6. examples include Richard III or Henry V

7. examples include "Something is rotten in the state of Denmark;"
"To be or not to be—that is the question;"
"A horse, a horse, my kingdom for a horse;"
"You're going to eat me out of house and home;"
"The green-eyed monster"

8. d	9. a	10. c	11. b
12. d	13. d	14. b	15. true
16. false	17. true	18. false	19. true

20. Macbeth and Lady Macbeth both had terrible nightmares. Macbeth saw Banquo's ghost. Lady Macbeth started walking in her sleep and rubbing her hands as if she were washing them, and she eventually died of a guilty conscience.

Chapter 40 Test

1. Virginia
2. Roanoke Island
3. Virginia Dare
4. Croatoan
5. c
6. b
7. a
8. c
9. d
10. b
11. c
12. d
13. false
14. true
15. false
16. true
17. false
18. Queen Elizabeth was interested in North America because she did not want Spain to become more important than England. Spain already had colonies in Central and South America and in the land that now belongs to Florida. If Spain took over North America, the Spanish Empire would become the largest and most powerful in the world.

Chapter 41 Test

1. Spanish & Portuguese
2. English
3. John Cabot
4. England
5. St. John's
6. Canada
7. b
8. a
9. c
10. b
11. a
12. b
13. c
14. c
15. true
16. true
17. false
18. true
19. true
20. The fishermen who settled in Newfoundland only stayed in their colony during the spring and summer because it was too cold during the winter. Huge storms came during the winter that would cover the island with ice and snow.

Chapter 42 Test

1. Spain
2. England
3. Spanish Armada
4. Francis Drake
5. b
6. d
7. b
8. b
9. d
10. b
11. b
12. d
13. false
14. false
15. true
16. The king of Spain was annoyed by English ships that kept sailing into Spanish waters. English traders were making money by selling slaves to the West Indies. English explorers were trying to settle land in North America that the king wanted for himself. Sometimes English ships stopped Spanish ships that were loaded with gold and robbed them.